Larry -

Just a note to tell
I am very proud of how much you
love God!!

Your friend,
Bruce

about

JAMES & JUDE

A Commentary

by

Pastor Bruce Ball

about JAMES and JUDE© 2018 / Pastor Bruce Ball
about JAMES and JUDE© is part of the series, 'about THE BIBLE©'
All Worldwide Rights Reserved

ISBN- 97-8179189491-7

AmCit-Ball Publishing©

DEDICATION

My dedication to this book is short and to the point. I thank my wife, Diana, for giving me the time and help as I studied, pieced together the information and then wrote this book.

But as much as I thank her, I thank the Lord Jesus Christ most of all, for it was He who loved me enough to wait until I realized my great need for Him, and then for taking me from the path I wanted to go and guiding me to where He wanted me to go, replacing my selfish desires with His Godly desires.

Thank You, LORD!

PREFACE

My desire is that each person who reads this book will come to the realization that it is Jesus Christ, the Son of God, who is our *only* pathway to Heaven. Let me explain my reasoning for saying that.

We must either believe the Bible in entirety, or we believe that none of it matters to us at all. And if we do claim to believe it, we must believe that it I 100% correct, as written, with no errors contained in it at all.

And if we believe it is correct, we are left with no other belief but to believe that, as the Bible claims, Jesus Christ is the Son of God who was sent from Heaven to be our spiritual Savior.

And so, if we are of the belief that the holy Bible is correct in what it says, we are left with no other alternative but to realize that the many beliefs that are present today that claim Jesus is NOT who the Bible says He is, or claim there are other ways to Heaven … well, according to the Bible, those beliefs are very wrong and all who subscribe to them are in danger of being hell bound on the day of their Judgment.

I say this, not as an elitist or one who excludes, but as one who truly cares about the future of others and is trying to show others the truth, according to the bible.

With a very thankful heart,

Pastor Bruce Ball

TABLE of CONTENTS

INTRODUCTION TO JAMES

There are two men who were half-brothers of Jesus who were leaders of the early church, and each wrote a book in the New Testament. One is James, and the other man is Jude.

And, with the book of JAMES, we are encountering a new group of New Testament books. JAMES and JUDE are called the "General Epistles" because they are not addressed to any specific individuals or churches as were Paul's letters.

JUDE only has one page, and JAMES only has five chapters. Do not let the short length of these books fool you, as each one is full of Godly information that every Christian needs to know!

Since neither are very long books, and since both authors were a sibling of our Lord Jesus, I have put them together into one book for your reading ease.

Let us start with the book of JAMES. We know that the author of this book was a man by the name of James. We know this because it tells us that in

VERSE 1

"James, a servant of God and of the Lord Jesus Christ, to the twelve tribes scattered among the nations: Greetings."

The letter is addressed *"To the twelve tribes scattered among the nations."* This was an historic reference to the Jews who had been dispersed throughout the surrounding nations by various empires over the centuries.

James may also have used it as code for Jewish Christians forced out of Jerusalem during a time of persecution, like after Stephen's death (ACT 8:1).

He also was writing to young believers scattered over a large area who needed exhortation and spiritual advice. Now that we have established '*who*' wrote it, (a man named James), let's look at '*which*' James wrote the letter.

First, there was James, the son of Zebedee. He was the brother of the apostle John. He was one of the first to believe in the Lord Jesus and he was one of the apostles.

But King Herod had this man killed around 42 A.D. (see ACTS 12:2). And since this letter was written after he died, we know it could not have been written by him.

Another recognizable leader in the church was James, the half-brother of Jesus. Originally, this James did not believe in Jesus as Divine. In fact, as most siblings would, he thought his brother was a bit crazy.

Jewish Christians instantly accepted this book, so the author must have been instantly known to them. The most popular man in those days who was named James, was the half-brother of Jesus Christ. His writings showed much authority within the church, and if it has been another James, he would have had to explain which James he was.

After Jesus came back from the dead (see 1 CORINTHIANS 15:7), he met with his brother James, and from then on, James believed in the deity of Jesus being the Christ. He is, by nearly all accounts, proven to be the author of this letter.

The bible also tells us more information about Jesus and his siblings. One Sabbath, Jesus and his disciples went into the synagogue and Jesus began teaching. He was so decisive, the people there asked if he wasn't the son of the carpenter, Joseph.

VERSE 3

"Isn't this the carpenter? Isn't this Mary's son and the brother of James,

Joseph, Judas and Simon? Aren't his sisters here with us?" And they took offense at him."

There is nothing else said until after he arose from the dead and went to see his disciples. The apostle Paul explains the timeline this way:

1 CORINTHAINS 15:3-7

³ For what I received I passed on to you as of first importance that Christ died for our sins according to the Scriptures, ⁴ that he was buried, that he was raised on the third day according to the Scriptures, ⁵ and that he appeared to Cephas, and then to the Twelve.

⁶ After that, he appeared to more than five hundred of the brothers and sisters at the same time, most of whom are still living, though some have fallen asleep. ⁷ Then he appeared to James, then to all the apostles."

When Jesus was ascending up into heaven, he told his disciples to wait in Jerusalem until he sent the Holy Spirit to them. So, they gathered together in an upstairs room and waited as they were told to do.

Gathered with them, were Jesus' mother Mary and his brothers (see ACTS 1:14). It appears that, at some point after his death, all of his family members came to believe in him as the Christ and the Son of God.

If that is the background for this letter, it helps resolve the so-called conflict between James and Paul regarding salvation by faith (compare JAMES 2:14-26 with GALATIANS 3:1).

The focus of James is living out one's faith while Paul's focus was explaining that salvation is through faith. Paul says nothing else is needed to save us except living our lives in faith. James, on the other hand, taught that the faith that saves results in a change that can be seen in what we do.

James is a series of short messages that exhort and command us in the way to properly follow God and his law. He offers no clear progression or logical sequence to them. He gives practical teaching on living the Christian life.

The letter of James reminds us a bit of Proverbs in the OT and is as hard to outline. He paints pictures and illustrates with everyday circumstances and objects from nature.

James never actually quotes Jesus, but sounds a lot like him, especially in places like the Sermon on the Mount (see MATTHEW 5-7). But that should not surprise us too much if they grew up as brothers together.

So, with that basic information, we will journey forth into the book of JAMES.

CHAPTER 1

VERSE 1

"James, a servant of God and of the Lord Jesus Christ; to the twelve tribes scattered among the nations: Greetings."

James is a humble man. He could have opened this letter by immediately saying he was a brother to Jesus, but he chose to put it in proper perspective; he is a servant. If most of us were to write the first verse above, we would have identified ourselves as being a brother to Jesus Christ. James, however, is totally focused on his relationship with the LORD.

Even though this letter was written to the Jews who had been scattered abroad who believed in Jesus Christ, it is also for every generation of Christians since; as we have all been scattered throughout the nations – all over the world. James is welcoming all who will believe into the church.

VERSES 2-4

"² Consider it pure joy, my brothers and sisters, whenever you face trials of many kinds, ³ because you know that the testing of your faith produces perseverance. ⁴ Let perseverance finish its work so that you may be mature and complete, not lacking anything."

The Greek word for 'trial' is the same word used to describe the word 'temptation'. What God sends to us to help grow our faith (trials), Satan will try to use to exploit us to make us sin (temptation). So, in verse 2, James says consider it pure joy we are faced with trials, because we know that by having our faith tested, it just grows stronger!

God does not expect us to be full of happiness and joy just because we are having problems in life, but He does expect us to see how having problems can help us have deeper faith in the LORD, by trusting Him and relying upon Him. Let me see if I can explain it in this way: If you want your body to grow stronger, you must work so that your muscles can grow.

Likewise, if you want deeper and stronger faith, you must put your faith to work. The more you work your faith, the stronger it will get – just like muscles. And the best way to work your faith is when you are having problems.

Nobody can sit in a recliner and automatically grow stronger muscles, and nobody can grow stronger faith without having a reason to use it and make it stronger. And so, we do not delight in having problems just for the sake of having problems, but we do delight in that our problems can help us to develop a stronger faith in our LORD.

VERSES 5-8

"⁵ If any of you lacks wisdom, you should ask God, who gives generously to all without finding fault, and it will be given to you. ⁶ But when you ask, you must believe and not doubt, because the one who doubts is like a wave of the sea, blown and tossed by the wind. ⁷ That person should not expect to receive anything from the Lord. ⁸ Such a person is double-minded and unstable in all they do."

And, when we are going through a problem, we need to know how to act, so again, we rely on God to give us the wisdom we need in order to go through the problem as best we can.

God loves his children, and he wants the very best for us. When we ask, we can either ask in hope, or in belief. God only speaks truth, so if he says he will do something – he will do it.

So, as we pray for wisdom, pray in the belief that you know he will give it to you! Do not just hope he does because that is not real belief. If we do not truly believe, we will not receive anything.

James says if we ask without really believing that we will receive it, we don't have no idea what is happening any more than a person on the ocean knows which way the waves will toss him. And God even goes so far as to say that person is unstable in everything in their lives.

In the Greek, James describes those who do not have solid belief in God answering their prayers as having two minds. It is like their trying to serve two different people at the same time and not being able to be loyal to one or the other because they are confused.

What I do when praying for something is to thank God for it, "even before I see any evidences of my getting it." And I try to actually see myself with the answer already given!

Again, and this is so important it bears repeating! All who feel the need of anything must ask God for it. He will answer the prayers of those who ask for it. But they must believe that he will give them what they are asking for before they can expect to get anything.

God is kind and generous. His desire is to give to you everything you need, and to give it in abundance for you; without limit, for all that they need.

Never be afraid to ask our loving Heavenly Father for whatever it is you need. God is always prepared to listen to you. In DANIEL, the angel came to Daniel and said God had herd his prayer the very instant Daniel began to pray! (See DANIEL 9:23 and 10:12).

And as far as being afraid you are asking God for help too often, 1 THESSALONIANS 5:17 tells us to NEVER STOP PRAYING! We are to be in constant communication with God. That will help our faith grow stronger in him and it will help us have a more holy life.

"⁹ Believers in humble circumstances ought to take pride in their high position. ¹⁰ But the rich should take pride in their humiliation - since they will pass away like a wild flower. ¹¹ For the sun rises with scorching heat and withers the plant; its blossom falls and its beauty is destroyed. In the same way, the rich will fade away even while they go about their business."

In verse, 9 James wants to encourage the poor brothers and sisters to fully trust in God. Because of their poor and humble situations, they might feel as if they are not important to God, but their hope for a better future is only found in their faith and belief in God.

The word "poor" and "humble" do not necessarily mean having little money. Those words also describe the spiritual condition of a person.

No matter what a person's financial situation in life, or even their position in life, a person can find pure joy just by having Christ Jesus as their personal Savior! If a person has allowed their life to be guided by Jesus Christ instead of their own self-interests, they actually have a place of high honor with God, and that is something they can consider with pure joy!

If a person relies upon Jesus Christ and looks to the future, then what they see should be pleasing to them – even if their earthly life seems hard and difficult.

They will receive from God all that he has promised to those who love him. They will be with Christ for all of eternity and they will share with him the riches of heaven.

The main problem is that some people do not look to the future, but only look at today. And when they want something, they tend to want it right now – on their terms and in their way.

Verse 10 explains that even the rich need to know that Jesus

Christ is the One whom they need to serve. Rich Christians must not be proud of what they own, but instead should be grateful that God has allowed them to own it. They must not be proud of the power that they have, but they must learn to use it the way God wants them to use it.

And everyone, even the rich, must be humble and realize that just because they have been blessed with having more than someone else, they are no better than anyone else. Their earthly wealth and position mean absolutely nothing to God, as God only looks at how they have used what they have for the benefit of others.

James writes about the beauty of a wildflower and how it lives and quickly dies. What seems so very long to us is but a brief moment to God. So we need to realize that even though our lives may seem long to us, in reality it is very short. But what we do in this life will be with us throughout eternity.

Our tendency is to put all our faith on what we have now, but God wants us to use this life as a way of properly preparing to be with him throughout eternity. We came into this world without any worldly possessions, and we will leave with just our Godly faith. Let us do all we can to protect it above everything else we might have or desire.

VERSES 12-15

"12 Blessed is the one who perseveres under trial because, having stood the test, that person will receive the crown of life that the Lord has promised to those who love him. 13 When tempted, no one should say, "God is tempting me." For God cannot be tempted by evil, nor does he tempt anyone;

"14 but each person is tempted when they are dragged away by their own evil desire and enticed. 15 Then, after desire has conceived, it gives birth to sin; and sin, when it is full-grown, gives birth to death."

The bible tells us that we will all have good days and bad days.

MATTHEW 5:45

"God causes his sun to rise on the evil and the good, and sends rain on the righteous and the unrighteous."

In verse 12, above, we are told that even though we will have bad days and experience many trials, we are to spiritually persevere through them so that we will prove ourselves worthy of receiving the 'crown of life' that God wants to reward us with.

Not fully understanding what is meant in verse 12 by receiving the crown of life, you may feel as if that isn't really important. Let me say that once you get to heaven you will think it very important.

In heaven, the crown we receive will determine what we will be doing. It could determine the number of cities we will reign over. (see LUKE 19:11-27).

Our first tendency when we experience a problem is to try and take care of it quickly – by ourselves! Generally, it is only after we have tried everything to contain the problem (and failed) that we seek God's help. We should do all we can to go to God first, and then let him direct our efforts.

It will only be those who walk through their troubles with God that will have the real joy of life. By their actions, they will have proven their trust in God and at the same will have grown their faith.

Something else that is common to man is that when we fail, it is always easier for us to blame it on someone else. In reality, the only one who bears the responsibility for our failures is ourselves!

Some even blame God, saying he is tempting them or for some other reason has turned his back on them. But the truth is, God is holy and righteous, and even though he might test us (for our benefits) he will never tempt us, for temptation is from Satan. God has no desire that any person should do wrong things.

The source of any temptation comes only from the desires and the weaknesses of our human nature. Those who sin have no real excuse other than that is what they chose to do at the time.

What we must ask ourselves is how we think God will react to our choice. Will he reward us for it, or will he punish us for it? Again, he puts the decision to sin or not directly upon our own shoulders.

Satan will entice us to commit sin, but he cannot force us to commit the sin. Our sin begins when we say "yes" to the desire and the sin blossoms into ungodliness when we act upon the sin.

ROMANS 6:23, in part says;

"… the wages of sin is death …"

In this case, "death" refers to "spiritual death". When we choose sin over God, we begin to die spiritually and if we do not repent and seek his forgiveness, we will go to hell when we die the physical death.

Some people ask how such a good God could send anyone to hell. Well, he doesn't send anyone to hell. They send themselves by the decisions they make to not live for God. And, when we tell God to leave us alone so we can live our lives the way we want to, he honors our request.

But when God leaves, he also takes his salvation with him. We must realize this. There are a lot of people, and even some churches that believe everyone will eventually go to heaven. My question is if they go "eventually", where do they hang out until they go to heaven?

VERSES 16-18

"16 Don't be deceived, my dear brothers and sisters. 17 Every good and perfect gift is from above, coming down from the Father of the heavenly lights, who does not change like shifting shadows. 18 He chose to give us birth through the word of truth that we might be a kind of first fruits of all he created."

Let me reemphasize, God does not tempt us and he has nothing to do with our being tempted. This comes from our own desire to do or to have things that are not connected to God.

Reading verse 16, it appears that those who James was speaking also had the wrong idea that God sent them temptation.

In verse 17, we are told that God is not the author of bad things, but it also tells us that God does not change. He is, and always has been, the same God with the same holiness that he has right now. In fact, we are told that in another verse, too.

HEBREWS 13:8

"Jesus Christ is the same yesterday and today and forever."

God created us. He chose to love us. And just as a woman might give birth to a small and precious baby, God has offered us a spiritual "new birth" when we make the conscious choice of letting Jesus Christ be our Savior, and submitting our own will over to his will for us.

In the Jewish religion, the first of the fruits belonged to God. We are to give God the first-fruits of all we get. That is our way of showing our love for God.

PROVERBS 3:9 tells us;

"Honor the Lord with your wealth and with the first-fruits of all your

crops."

What happens with you give to the church? A Godly church will take your gifts and use it to help others. They pay rent, utilities and other things just as you must do and they need income to do it with. Also, they purchase study materials and song books, equipment and must also pay salaries.

Granted, there are some churches who operate as a business-for-profit, but a true and Godly church helps others with all they have. And as far as we go; we are to give to our church (see MALACHI3:9-10).

If the church misuses our gifts, God will punish them, but will reward us for being faithful servants unto him.

VERSES 19-25

"19 My dear brothers and sisters, take note of this: Everyone should be quick to listen, slow to speak and slow to become angry, 20 because human anger does not produce the righteousness that God desires. 21 Therefore, get rid of all moral filth and the evil that is so prevalent and humbly accept the word planted in you, which can save you.

"22 Do not merely listen to the word, and so deceive yourselves. Do what it says. 23 Anyone who listens to the word but does not do what it says is like someone who looks at his face in a mirror 24 and, after looking at himself, goes away and immediately forgets what he looks like. 25 But whoever looks intently into the perfect law that gives freedom, and continues in it - not forgetting what they have heard, but doing it - they will be blessed in what they do."

James implores his audience to be quick to listen but slow to speak or become angry. Listening will increase their knowledge and understanding, but when we speak too quickly it is without giving ourselves enough time to really think about what we want to say, and when we get angry, it often leads us quickly away from the LORD. Also, by our listening, we can also hear what God is trying to say to us.

We are instructed to get rid of all moral filth! One good example of that is how some religions teach something other than what the bible says, yet say it is right and even Godly!

It will only be by listening with an intent heart, and without getting angry when the truth of God is presented to you, that you will actually be living for God.

Receiving the Word of God means more than just hearing the sound of the words; to receive it, we must actually put it to use in our lives. Make it active within us. DO WHAT IT SAYS!

If we do not actively make it a part of our lives and if we do not do what it says to do, then we receive no benefit from the LORD.

Some think that just listening to the Word will save them. That is like how some people think that just because they go to church they are Christians. Both of these ideas are wrong! We are Christians because we have let Christ become a part of our hearts.

And with him in our hearts, we now have a yearning desire to hear his word, and an equally yearning desire to put the Word into our lives and make it active.

VERSES 26-27

"26 Those who consider themselves religious and yet do not keep a tight rein on their tongues deceive themselves, and their religion is worthless. 27 Religion that God our Father accepts as pure and faultless is this: to look after orphans and widows in their distress and to keep oneself from being polluted by the world."

Many people consider themselves religious or think they are

good Christians for a variety of reasons, but it says in JAMES that if a person considers themselves to be like that but they not try and do as Jesus wants, their 'religion'

Those people who are harsh, or demeaning with their words may think that they are all right, but their 'religion' is nothing more than empty words. They say things that sound good. But, without good acts, their words are of no use. Their religion is vain and of no use because it fails to please God.

None of us are perfect, and God knows this. But what he expects from us is that we love his Son enough to try and be like him. That is what being "Christ-like" is all about – not just doing the things we know we should, but living the way we should so we can please God.

Basically, there are two main parts to living for God: The first is loving God with all your heart – just because that is what you choose to do.

The second part is trying to love others as God loves them. Love will always make you want to help and do good things for others, not shun them or walk past them when they need help. A pure religion that pleases God is one that comforts and helps others as you live to please Jesus Christ.

And there is something else, too. Our God wants us to do all we can to avoid evil, shun temptations, and truly rely on Him. Those people who know God like this will do good works. He is not only their God but he is their Father. They have become his children by trusting in the Lord Jesus.

CHAPTER 2

One thing it seem all humans have in common is our tendency to play favorites. We choose one person over another based on many things, but no matter why we do it, it is all based upon our selfish thoughts of them. As we will find out in this chapter, God hates this!

VERSES 1-4

"¹ My brothers and sisters, believers in our glorious Lord Jesus Christ must not show favoritism. ² Suppose a man comes into your meeting wearing a gold ring and fine clothes, and a poor man in filthy old clothes also comes in. ³ If you show special attention to the man wearing fine clothes and say, "Here's a good seat for you," but say to the poor man, "You stand there" or "Sit on the floor by my feet," ⁴ have you not discriminated among yourselves and become judges with evil thoughts?

God says that all real believers are members of his household. (See EPHESIANS 2:19). That makes us all spiritual brothers and sisters in God's family. That is why James refers to other believers as "brothers and sisters".

And he begins in verse 1 by telling us to stop showing favoritism. He says we "must" stop doing this! And then, he gives us an illustration about two men coming to a dinner.

One man is rich and the other poor, and we give the best seat to the rich man. James says we are showing favoritism and in so doing, we are becoming a judge over them.

In God's eyes, we are all worth the same, whether we are male or female, rich or poor, or one race over another. To him, there are two basic types of people; those who do believe in Jesus and those who do not.

Jesus came from heaven, being having the most to offer than anyone else who has ever lived, yet he put it all aside when he stepped from his royal throne and came down here to be born naked in an animal's manger! Should we show favoritism against him?

He did not have respect for people because of their wealth or power. He is for us the example of how we should respect all people. We should respect them, no matter how poor they may be.

VERSES 5-7

"5 Listen, my dear brothers and sisters: Has not God chosen those who are poor in the eyes of the world to be rich in faith and to inherit the kingdom he promised those who love him? 6 But you have dishonored the poor. Is it not the rich who are exploiting you? Are they not the ones who are dragging you into court? 7 Are they not the ones who are blaspheming the noble name of him to whom you belong?"

What James is saying is so important that they must listen to it. This false respect we give to others is unwise. We tend to show this fake feeling of respect to those we know do not deserve it. The next few verses explain why.

Few people in the early church came from the rich or ruling class. Today is different in that some leaders are very wealthy and some are even wealthy due to how they have exploited their ministries.

But, just like in the days of JAMES, even today most Christians are not wealthy. God chose people who were considered poor to be rich - in faith. God has not limited his choice to poor people, but they have been his first choice.

I think because they are more willing to be humble and listen to Him than those who spend all their time focusing on their riches. They depend on God more so than the rich. They do not depend on what they are or the things that they own. The poor who believe in Jesus are rich in that they have - a place in the kingdom of God. This home in heaven is ready for those who love God. He did not promise this as a reward for their love but as a reward for their loving His Son to submit their will to His.

In this illustration, James is saying those who hosted the dinner insulted everyone by not giving the poor man respect for who he was instead of what he had.

Those who focus on what they have or what they want to have, prove themselves selfish and disrespectful – both towards their fellow man and to God, who has given them all they have in the first place.

VERSES 8-13

"8 If you really keep the royal law found in Scripture, "Love your neighbor as yourself," you are doing right. 9 But if you show favoritism, you sin and are convicted by God as lawbreakers. 10 For whoever keeps the whole law and yet stumbles at just one point is guilty of breaking all of it. 11 For he who said, "You shall not commit adultery," also said, "You shall not murder." If you do not commit adultery but do commit murder, you have become a lawbreaker."

"12 Speak and act as those who are going to be judged by the law that gives freedom, 13 because judgment without mercy will be shown to anyone who has not been merciful. Mercy triumphs over judgment."

Wow! These verses are very clear and do not need any explanation or translation. God's law instructs us to treat everyone with respect, kindness and without any favoritism. If we do that, we are safe on Judgment Day.

However, if we do not do these things, then on Judgment Day we shall receive the punishment that lawbreakers deserve.

You have the right to disagree with what another says or does, but you do not have the right to be nasty of heart in how you handle it. We follow the Apostle Paul's instruction to handle everything in a loving way. (See 1 Corinthians 16:14).

VERSES 14-20

"14 What good is it, my brothers and sisters, if someone claims to have faith but has no deeds? Can such faith save them? 15 Suppose a brother or a sister is without clothes and daily food. 16 If one of you says to them, "Go in peace; keep warm and well fed," but does nothing about their physical needs, what good is it? 17 In the same way, faith by itself, if it is not accompanied by action, is dead.

"18 But someone will say, "You have faith; I have deeds." Show me your faith without deeds, and I will show you my faith by my deeds. 19 You believe that there is one God. Good! Even the demons believe that - and shudder. 20 You foolish person, do you want evidence that faith without deeds is useless?"

Many are so mixed up when it comes to the subject of faith and deeds. Faith is what you believe in. Deeds are the actions you do. We need to be aware, first of all, that our deeds will most often reveal what our heart feel.

Are we doing something just because we know we should, or because someone expects us to do it? Or, are we doing something because we really and truly want to do it?

Read verse 20 again! Is faith without deeds good enough? No! If we have true faith in God, through Jesus Christ, then we will desire to do good things. So real faith is doing things for others for no other reason than because you really want to.

VERSES 21-26

"21 Was not our father Abraham considered righteous for what he did when he offered his son Isaac on the altar? 22 You see that his faith and his

actions were working together, and his faith was made complete by what he did. ²³ *And the scripture was fulfilled that says, "Abraham believed God, and it was credited to him as righteousness," and he was called God's friend.* "²⁴ *You see that a person is considered righteous by what they do and not by faith alone.*

²⁵ *In the same way, was not even Rahab the prostitute considered righteous for what she did when she gave lodging to the spies and sent them off in a different direction?* ²⁶ *As the body without the spirit is dead, so faith without deeds is dead."*

Abraham had true and lasting faith. When God told him to move away, he did so. He did not hesitate or argue with God. He had instant obedience and moved – even though God had not told him where to move yet!

That is faith. When we believe enough to have God's instructions become a way of life for us, we have faith. It is like the old farmer who once said, *"God said it; I believe it; and that settles it."*

It is not faith when you feel required to do good deeds to show others how faithful you are. It is only real faith when you do good deeds because you know Jesus wants you to, and you want to please him.

CHAPTER 3

VERSE 1

"Not many of you should become teachers, my fellow believers, because you know that we who teach will be judged more strictly."

Did you know that God will hold teachers of Scriptures to a higher degree of accountability when it comes to teaching them to others?

That is because teachers have an extraordinary influence on what a student believes? It does not matter the subject, when a student listens to a teacher, that student trusts that the teacher knows the subject backwards and forwards

And that student will take to heart what he or she is being taught. Now, if what they are being taught is wrong, they will take that wrong information with them and it will eventually cause them trouble. That is why God warns us not to be too eager to be a teacher of the bible.

VERSE 2 [New Living Translation©] (Tyndale House©)

"Indeed, we all make many mistakes. For if we could control our tongues, we would be perfect and could also control ourselves in every other way."

Even though God warns us about the pitfalls associated with teaching, and even though he holds teachers to a much higher degree of accountability than others, he has proven himself to be understandable and loving. He knows we all stumble and we must remember that he is quick to forgive.

The trick is to do your homework so that when you teach, you teach strictly according to what the bible says, and you have a heart to give God's absolute truth to students and not teach for any other reason.

That is how false gospels come about; some people purposely teach things that are not biblical, and they do so for purely selfish reasons.

For instance, ACTS 20:29-30 warns us;

"29 I know that after I leave, savage wolves will come in among you and will not spare the flock. 30 Even from your own number men will arise and distort the truth in order to draw away disciples after them."

False teachers are called "savage wolves" because what they do is just as deadly to us (spiritually), as what savage wolves do to a person (physically) when they attack them.

VERSES 3-4

"3 When we put bits into the mouths of horses to make them obey us, we can turn the whole animal. 4 Or take ships as an example. Although they are so large and are driven by strong winds, they are steered by a very small rudder wherever the pilot wants to go."

The size of something does not necessarily relate to its power or importance. James gives two examples above; the horse's bit and the rudder of a large ship.

Both are relatively small in relation to what they have control over, but both can, and do, control the larger object. And now, James turns the attention onto the small part of the body that oft-times will lead a person to make hellish decisions – the tongue.

VERSES 5-6

"5 Likewise, the tongue is a small part of the body, but it makes great boasts. Consider what a great forest is set on fire by a small spark. 6 The

tongue also is a fire, a world of evil among the parts of the body. It corrupts the whole body, sets the whole course of one's life on fire, and is itself set on fire by hell."

In relation to our whole bodies, our tongues are very small, but we sometimes do not realize just how powerful they are! The words we utter can bring about good and bad, and they can build or tear down. And words can actually change the course of nations.

And those words are controlled by our tongues. And our tongues are controlled by our hearts.

James is not saying that we should not talk. He is arguing for control of the tongue, and the wise use of words. The mind and the heart control what we say. With the help of the Spirit of Christ, we can have that control. Then we can use our tongue to bless people instead of curse them.

To illustrate his teaching even more, James considers how a great forest can be utterly destroyed by a fire; a fire which was started by a very small spark. And the whole body can be destroyed by the use of our very small tongues.

It is the fire; a fire that comes straight from hell. That is what makes the tongue so dangerous.

Let me offer my own illustration. We have all experienced what it is like to be very angry at another person. The first thing we tend to do is say harsh things (or worse) and all of it is directed either at the person or at what that person is doing or saying.

Are the feelings behind those words we say good or bad? Do you think they come from love or hate (frustration, negatives, etc?) And who do you think is behind those feelings? It certainly is not God. And we can literally destroy the person we are saying them to.

Karen Carpenter, the sister in the hit group 'The Carpenters' in the 1970's read an article where the author called her "fat", among other negative things. It affected her so badly that she ended up starving herself to death!

VERSES 7-12

"7 All kinds of animals, birds, reptiles and sea creatures are being tamed and have been tamed by mankind, 8 but no human being can tame the tongue. It is a restless evil, full of deadly poison.

"9 With the tongue we praise our Lord and Father, and with it we curse human beings, who have been made in God's likeness. 10 Out of the same mouth come praise and cursing. My brothers and sisters, this should not be. 11 Can both fresh water and salt water flow from the same spring? 12 My brothers and sisters, can a fig tree bear olives, or a grapevine bear figs? Neither can a salt spring produce fresh water."

Humans can control all kinds of animals, birds, snakes and fishes. When God made the earth, he gave Adam the authority over all other living creatures.

But when man chose sin over obedience to God, something happened. We gave a part of our hearts and minds over to be influenced by Satan. So now, even though we still have ultimate dominion over other creatures, we can no longer control them.

And the one living creature we seem to not have control over, without God's explicit help, is …. ourselves! We might be able to do many things, but we do not seem to be able to control our own tongues!

The tongue is like an animal in a cage. It will not rest and it always tries to get free. We can keep an animal like this so that it cannot escape. But this is not possible with the tongue. It is never at rest long enough for us to control it. It is ready at all times to break out into evil.

It is not that it never speaks good, but it often speaks evil. It is like a snake full of poison that can kill. Evil words are worse than the bite of animals and the poison of snakes.

In verse 9, it tells us that *"With the tongue we praise our Lord and Father, and with it we curse human beings, who have been made in God's likeness."* Now think about that for a moment. Does it make any sense at all to use the same mouth to bless and to curse? God does not want us to do that, but Satan does. Which one are we willing to obey and succumb to?

God made men to be like himself spiritually and that image remains in people. It is what helps us to know what we ought to do. It helps us hear God. However, sin has damaged that image of God in us. Oh, his image is still there, but it is now tucked away deep inside, and the evil of our sin tries to keep it hidden.

We ought not to curse people whom God made to be like him. As God made all humans in his own image, to curse a person is, in effect, to curse God. So to use the same tongue to bless God and to curse people is wrong and is a personal insult to God for us to do that.

MATTHEW 12:34 tells us where these evil things come from:

"You brood of vipers, how can you, who are evil, say anything good? For the mouth speaks what the heart is full of."

The bad things we say come from the bad things in our hearts. This is a very dangerous thing MATTHEW warns us of. This subject is so serious, it is carried throughout the bible.

PROVERBS 2:23 gives us that same warning!

"Above all else, guard your heart, for everything you do flows from it."

There are more, but the last example I will use to show how very important it is we try to tame our tongues, is seen in:

"A good man brings good things out of the good stored up in his heart, and an evil man brings evil things out of the evil stored up in his heart. For the mouth speaks what the heart is full of."

People say what is in their hearts and minds. Mature Christians will work very hard to control what they think and say. The Holy Spirit gives them power so that they can control their tongues. They will praise God and they will also speak well of people. But so often, they fail to make use of the control that he gives.

It is wrong to bless and curse with the same tongue. Christians should not mix good words with evil talk like this. To curse men in that way makes the blessing just empty words and of no use. People try to honor God, but they think and speak evil about people at the same time.

The land where James lived did not have much rain. A town or village may have to depend on springs or wells for their water. Sweet water and bitter water cannot come out of the same spring. It can have only one type of water; sweet or bitter.

Sweet water is fresh and good to drink. Bitter water is not good to drink and it can make you very sick. Sweet water is free of impurities, while bitter water can be the home of many germs and diseases.

Figs, olives and grapes were the three most common fruits the farmers grew in that area. The fig tree produced figs. The olive tree produced olives. And the grape vines produced grapes. In nature, a tree can only produce the fruit it is. It is a fact of nature that like produces like.

Similarly, a fountain has one type of water. It will have sweet water or it will have bitter water. It cannot have both. Out of the mouth of a good person, there should come only one kind of word – the word that is stored up in the heart. It is abhorrent to nature for us to speak both kinds of words.

VERSES 13-18

"13 Who is wise and understanding among you? Let them show it by their good life, by deeds done in the humility that comes from wisdom.

14 But if you harbor bitter envy and selfish ambition in your hearts, do not boast about it or deny the truth. 15 Such "wisdom" does not come down from heaven but is earthly, unspiritual, and demonic. 16 For where you have envy and selfish ambition, there you find disorder and every evil practice.

"17 But the wisdom that comes from heaven is first of all pure; then peace-loving, considerate, submissive, full of mercy and good fruit, impartial and sincere. 18 Peacemakers who sow in peace reap a harvest of righteousness."

James starts out in verse 13 by asking which one of them has wisdom or knowledge. Notice how he does not want to know which ones think they are important or who think they have all the answers. Wisdom and knowledge only come from God. He is asking which ones rely on the LORD for what they have and what they do with it.

Also, keep in mind that knowledge and wisdom are not the same. Knowledge lets us know how something works, or what it is intended for. It lets us know about the situation or object. Wisdom is quite different. Wisdom lets us know how to use the knowledge we have. A person who is actively trying to live for God will strive to have both knowledge and wisdom.

We show our wisdom, not so much by saying things, but by doing the things we do. People see us doing something and they can tell by the way we do it and the expression on our face whether we are doing it simply because we have to, or because we want to. When we want to do things, especially things that will benefit others, we are showing Godly wisdom.

You will show others the basic type of person you are by the way you have chosen to live. Others can tell if you are a boisterous person, a bragging person, or a loving person. A loving person will most often exhibit a lifestyle of meekness.

Some people equate meekness with weakness. That is far from the truth! There is an old saying that explains this very well: *"If you think meek is weak, try being meek for a week."*

Having a meek heart is just another way of saying a person has the heart of God. It is full of love for his fellow man and will always try to do those things that help others rather than just build himself up. It takes a person of real character to be meek.

Those who seek to be honored themselves are not wise, loving or meek. They are insecure and need attention to verify their self-worth. They are jealous of others and think others are better than themselves. They work hard for their own advantage. Their attitudes are not good and they will cause bad relationships in and out of the church because they must be the center of attention.

Where people are proud and have selfish ambition, there is no true wisdom. There is only a false wisdom that has nothing to do with God. It does not come from above, it comes from self. To have wisdom from above is to have the wisdom that God gives.

Verse 16 informs us that human wisdom is proud and jealous. It is the cause of disagreement, not peace and it certainly has nothing to do with the LORD. When a person is focused on themselves instead of on God, they tend to destroy life with God.

They do nothing to help Christians and even less to offer any real help to the church. These works just destroy the unity that should be between people.

There is only one true wisdom, and it only comes from God. It is a different kind of wisdom. It is a gift. James has previously described what this wisdom is *not*. Now, he shows what it *is*. He uses seven words to describe it.

1. It is *pure* and clean. It holy, as God himself is holy.

2. It is a *peaceful*. It brings people closer together not put space between them

3. It is *gentle*. It knows the weakness of others and helps them. It does not blame.

4. It is *reasonable*. It will listen to what other people say.

5. It is full of *mercy*. It offers help to the suffering. And it has sympathy for all those who are sad. It has the pity and the love to do good for them and all people.

6. It is *fair* to all. It shows respect for all people. It does not show favoritism and is always ready to go good.

7. It is real and *sincere*. It is honest. It does not pretend.

Above all, it can be described as Godly in nature. Verse 18 says, Those who have this wisdom do good works, and those good works result in blessings and peace. They are like seeds that grow up into a plant. The fruit of that plant is righteousness and the soil in which it grows is peace.

Peace means a right relationship with other people and with God. If this does not exist, there can be no true righteousness.

CHAPTER 4

"¹ What causes fights and quarrels among you? Don't they come from your desires that battle within you? ² You desire but do not have, so you kill. You covet but you cannot get what you want, so you quarrel and fight. You do not have because you do not ask God. ³ When you ask, you do not receive, because you ask with wrong motives, that you may spend what you get on your pleasures.

"⁴ You adulterous people, don't you know that friendship with the world means enmity against God? Therefore, anyone who chooses to be a friend of the world becomes an enemy of God. ⁵ Or do you think Scripture says without reason that he jealously longs for the spirit he has caused to dwell in us? ⁶ But he gives us more grace. That is why Scripture says: "God opposes the proud, but shows favor to the humble."

There were problems in the early church where there should have only been peace. James asks the readers to think about what the real source of the disagreements were. There were arguments and quarrels in the church. There were angry words and they said bad things to one another and about one another.

I am sure they had many reasons for their attitudes but the real cause of these quarrels was their own desires. They each wanted what pleased themselves. When they could not agree on what they wanted to do, there was trouble.

I have often heard where there have been churches today that either split up, dissolved, or had great acrimony due to nothing more than what color the new carpet should be! I do not think God is pleased with attitudes such as these. When people put their own desires above other people's desires, there will be struggling, hating and fighting.

By our nature, our pleasures tend to rule our lives. We need the grace of God to make us free from this selfish attitude. And when we allow our own desires to have first place in our lives, we will not be able to do what God wants us to do. Our desire ought to be to do what God wants us to do. And we should desire to be what he wants us to be.

Verse 2 explains that our selfish desire to have what we want is our cause for ill will. James goes on to say that we do not have what we want, because we do not go to God and ask him for what we want. Who knows – maybe if we did go to God, he would take away those desires of ours that do not honor him and replace them with desire that do honor him.

God is ready to answer the prayers of those who ask for what is right. Righteous people ask for what God wants to give. So he hears them. Some of these people prayed but with wrong desires. They did not receive what they asked for because their requests did not care what God wanted, they just cared for what they wanted.

God is not the author of selfishness and evil, so he will not answer prayers that are selfish and evil.

When a person is not faithful in thought to God, but on himself it I a sin. And God looks at this just like he looks at it when people commit adultery. It is an act of unfaithfulness. It is an act of pure sin.

James is saying they were not faithful to Jesus Christ. They did not love God as they should, but instead loved the things of the world. Those who share the values of the world are not faithful to God. That is the world apart from God. The things of the world include all that opposes God and his rules.

James is thinking here about those pleasures and aims that draw people away from God. It is the desire for wealth; power and pleasure that governs those of the world. They refuse the rule of God.

Desire for the things of the world is friendship with the world. That is the same feelings we have when we are embarrassed to share the gospel because of what others might say to us. Maybe it is time to think about what God wants instead of what the world around us wants.

By its nature, friendship with the world is against God. He who is a friend of the world, becomes an enemy of God. Christians cannot love God and be friends with the world.

They have to choose between God and the world. They can be friends either with the world or with God, not both.

MATTHEW 6:24 puts it like this:

"No one can serve two masters. Either you will hate one and love the other, or you will be devoted to one and despise the other. You cannot serve both God and money."

And, we cannot serve the people who live in this world so we can make them happy with us and serve the God of Creation who wants us to be happy with him. It's all about choices and choosing which one you want to serve.

God has sent the Holy Spirit to live in us. The Holy Spirit wants us to put God first in our lives; in every situation and all the time. He opposes everything in us that would draw us away from God. He desires us to be faithful and to love God and the Lord Jesus Christ.

God is a jealous God, not in the way we feel jealousy, but in the way that He wants us to worship him. He loves us. And he does not want us to love anyone more than we love him. The word 'jealous' comes from a word meaning 'burning heat'. This shows the strong desire with which God longs for our love.

Only the loving help of God can make us able to accept the love of God. It is his love for us that compels him to extend his grace to us. So, even though God seems to require a lot from us, he freely gives us all the help we need to do what he wants. That is full grace given in full love.

God opposes those who have prideful attitudes, because pride is a self-centered word. God does not want us to focus on us, but on him. Prideful people do not love God, and they refuse to obey him. They are friends of the world.

And so, they are enemies of God. They have turned away from their Maker and so he has turned away from them. The proud do not think they need God's loving help.

But when something bad happens in their lives, the first thing they do is blame God for allowing it. They do not realize God did not cause the bad, all he did was honor their request for God to leave them alone, which he did. But when you tell God you do not need or want him, he will go but when he goes, he takes his blessings and safe covering with him – leaving you very vulnerable.

VERSES 7-10

"⁷ Submit yourselves, then, to God. Resist the devil, and he will flee from you. ⁸ Come near to God and he will come near to you. Wash your hands, you sinners, and purify your hearts, you double-minded. ⁹ Grieve, mourn and wail. Change your laughter to mourning and your joy to gloom. ¹⁰ Humble yourselves before the Lord, and he will lift you up."

Humble your heart to God. Worship him. Receive his Son, Jesus as your Savior. God gives help to the humble.

James is saying that as they give control of their lives over to God, he will give the power, through the Holy Spirit, that will enable them to fight and defeat the evil one. Then James tells them to oppose the devil. These two actions are two sides of the same thing.

They must turn to God and they must turn against the devil. The devil knows that his only hope is to draw Christians away from their trust in God. The cause of their failure is often that they are proud, and Satan appeals to their pride. As strong as the devil is, humble Christians to God can defeat him through Christ. As we say 'no' to his temptations, he has to go away from us.

James tells the believers of his day that it is their personal desires that has drawn them away from God. In wanting to please themselves, they have left God behind. They are still God's people, but they have begun to ignore him and now seem like strangers to him.

They had to repent and again seek his face in their lives. God never refuses to forgive those who repent and turn to him. God is so good and kind to all those who come to him. As they approach God, he will come near to them.

In verse 8, James says to wash our hands (ask God to cleanse the sin from our lives to purify our hearts.) In other words, go to God and really focus on him. Ask him to forgive you and to help you submit to him.

Sinners do what God says not to do, or who refuse to do what God says to do. And they do it with stubborn minds and prideful hearts. Those with two souls (or minds) are those who want to be Godly, but they do not want to let loose of the things of this world, either. You must make a choice as to who you want to be with more – God or the world. It is your choice to make, too.

The washing of hands was part of the ceremony of worship It was to make a person fit to come near to God.

PSALM 24:3-4 says this about washing of hands.

"3 Who may ascend into the hill of the LORD? And who may stand in His holy place? 4 He who has clean hands and a pure heart, who has not lifted up his soul to falsehood and has not sworn deceitfully."

This means to repent and turn from their sin. They have to *choose* to follow God and not be afraid of what anyone else says or does.

JAMES 4:9 continues to say they should be sorry for their sins. They should be so sorry that it causes them to be very sad. They should weep because of what they have done. They should no longer laugh at and enjoy the things of the world.

Instead, as they think about their sins, they should be sad and unhappy. When they have come back to the Lord, then they will be able to laugh and be glad again. We must remember that the only thing the world can give us is temporary laughter or a small amount of temporary enjoyment. But if we are seeking real joy, the only place it will come from is with a very real and very sincere personal relationship with God, through Jesus Christ.

In verse 10, we are told to come to God with a humble heart. We are not the center of the universe. In relation to God, we are small and weak. Only those who come to God like this can know his blessings. God has promised to lift them up, to forgive them and to make them strong. Only those who come to God like this will ever know the future of heaven.

VERSES 11-12

"11 Do not speak against one another, brethren. He who speaks against a brother or judges his brother, speaks against the law and judges the law; but if you judge the law, you are not a doer of the law but a judge of it. 12 There is only one Lawgiver and Judge, the One who is able to save and to destroy; but who are you who judge your neighbor?"

James is writing that in the church, there were those who had said bad things about other Christians, unkind things and possibly even lies. He said they must stop doing it because they are brothers and sisters.

To speak against a Christian was against the same law that told them to love their brothers and sisters. They could not speak evil about other Christians and at the same time love them. The person, who speaks bad things about another person, acts as a judge of that person. Those who do this also speak against the law of God.

It is as if they say that God, and his law, does not matter at that moment in time. Their own ideas are to them more important than the law of God. But our *duty* to God is not to judge the law but to obey it. Those who judge will also be judged one day.

MATTHEW 7:1-2 [New Living Translation© (Tyndale House©)

¹ "Do not judge others, and you will not be judged. ² For you will be treated in the same way in you treat others. The standard you use in judging is the same standard by which you will be judged."

Everyone judges other people negatively at some time or other in their lives. Aren't we glad that we have a God who forgives us of our sins?

No person has the right to cast their own personal judgment on another – for any reason! There is only one person who can be the judge. That is God, who gave us the law in the first place. No man can put aside the law of God. It is for all people and for all time.

God is the only real judge, and he will judge us all by the same standard – his standard. He does not need, nor does he want, our help in judging.

VERSES 13-17

"13 Now listen, you who say, "Today or tomorrow we will go to this or that city, spend a year there, carry on business and make money." 14 Why,

you do not even know what will happen tomorrow. What is your life? You are a mist that appears for a little while and then vanishes. 15 Instead, you ought to say, "If it is the Lord's will, we will live and do this or that."

16 As it is, you boast in your arrogant schemes. All such boasting is evil. 17 If anyone, then, knows the good they ought to do and doesn't do it, it is sin for them."

James shows that it is a very bad mistake on our parts to plan our futures without having God in it. The Jews travelled quite often back then. Some would travel for the purpose of business. And so, using business as an example, James speaks about merchants who are in the church.

His illustration uses some merchants who are planning a trip. They say, *"We will go on the day that we decide. We will go to a certain city that we choose, and our plan is to stay there a year. We will trade there and we will make a profit."*

But they gave God no place in their plans. These merchants thought they could do as *they* have planned, without considering God in their plans at all. It was as if the future was in their own hands to control. But God alone knows the future and it makes no sense to plan without him. Planning for the future is good but it must be with God. God's plan is above all other plans.

Those merchants could never know just what their tomorrows would encounter. But rather than rely on the One who could get them through it safely, they ignored him and made all the plans for themselves.

This human life lasts only for a short time. The only certain thing is that at some point in time everyone will leave this earth.

In the morning, the mist covers the country. By noon it has all gone. Human life is like that. The use of the word 'mist' expresses the thought that life is short. Human life on earth is like a mist, or smoke. It is here for one short moment in time and gone the next.

Verse 15 does not tell them to not plan. It is good to plan, but when planning for the future, it is always best to go to God in prayer and ask him to let you know what he wants you to do.

The proud merchants were very confident in themselves. They were sure that by their own efforts they would succeed. Having confidence is good if you use it correctly. But having confidence in themselves like that, without even thinking about what God wants for you, is evil. To think that they could plan the future without God is sin against God. Only God can know what is to come.

Lastly, in verse 17, we see that sin is not just doing things that God has told us not to do, but it also includes not doing things God has told us to do.

CHAPTER 5

VERSES 1-6

"¹ Now listen, you rich people, weep and wail because of the misery that is coming on you! ² Your wealth has rotted, and moths have eaten your clothes. ³ Your gold and silver are corroded. Their corrosion will testify against you and eat your flesh like fire. You have hoarded wealth in the last days.

"⁴ Look! The wages you failed to pay the workers who mowed your fields are crying out against you. The cries of the harvesters have reached the ears of the Lord Almighty. ⁵ You have lived on earth in luxury and self-indulgence. You have fattened yourselves in the day of slaughter. ⁶ You have condemned and murdered the innocent one, who was not opposing you."

James starts this passage with a very strong warning to some rich people who have cheated people who they have employed. He tells them to be very frightened and sad about what is in store for them on the Day of Judgment.

And in verse 2, he begins to paint a very ugly picture of what their love of money has done to them. He says it has caused them to rot. He says their clothes will not last, and neither will their wealth.

In verse 4, James tells them of how they cheat others. He says they do not pay them properly, if at all, while they themselves live in total luxury. Do we have the same problem today? Of course we do! James tells us that people like that are just fattening themselves up for the slaughter; meaning that each sin they commit just adds to the weight of their future judgment.

VERSES 7-11

"⁷ Be patient, then, brothers and sisters, until the Lord's coming. See

how the farmer waits for the land to yield its valuable crop, patiently waiting for the autumn and spring rains. ⁸ You too, be patient and stand firm, because the Lord's coming is near. ⁹ Don't grumble against one another, brothers and sisters, or you will be judged. The Judge is standing at the door!

"¹⁰ Brothers and sisters, as an example of patience in the face of suffering, take the prophets who spoke in the name of the Lord. ¹¹ As you know, we count as blessed those who have persevered. You have heard of Job's perseverance and have seen what the Lord finally brought about. The Lord is full of compassion and mercy."

James now speaks to his Christian brothers and sisters about their not getting impatient. He tells them to have patience until God acts on their behalf. They may have to suffer while they wait, but the LORD will punish those who have caused them to suffer.

In the meantime, Christians must leave the judgement of the rich to God. They must not do what is wrong against those who do wrong to them. This does not mean that we should not speak out for justice, but when we do, do so in a Godly way and not in a vengeful way.

Before we go on and talk about the LORD's coming, we must be sure we all understand about his return. That is the 2ⁿᵈ Coming of Christ. That is a totally different event than when he comes for the Rapture. Let me explain the difference.

When Jesus comes in the Rapture, the bible says he will be in the clouds (in the sky) and he will call all believers up to him. That includes both the believers who died as believers and those who are still living as believers. Here is how he will do it:

1 THESSALONIANS 4:16-17

"¹⁶ The LORD himself will come down from heaven, with a loud command, with the voice of the archangel and with the trumpet call of God,

44

and the dead in Christ will rise first. *¹⁷ After that, we who are still alive and are left will be caught up together with them in the clouds to meet the Lord in the air. And then, we will be with the Lord forever.*"

For God to be able to extend his punishment out on a sinful and rebellious world, he will first remove believers from the earth. He will use the Rapture to call us all up to heaven, and then he will spend the next seven-years (the End Times) dealing with the world and the Jews in particular.

Now, the 2ⁿᵈ Coming of Jesus is different. At the end of the seven-year period described in the previous paragraph, Jesus will come to earth to punish those who have rejected him. Notice how in the Rapture, he calls us up to meet him in the air. He does not come to earth.

In the 2ⁿᵈ Coming, he will come to earth and the bible tells us that he will stand upon the Mt. of Olives.

ZECHARIAH 14:4 tells us about that day.

"On that day, his feet will stand on the Mount of Olives, east of Jerusalem - and the Mount of Olives will be split in two from east to west, forming a great valley, with half of the mountain moving north and half moving south."

When he came to earth before, he came as a peacemaker, one who came to save. When he comes in the 2ⁿᵈ Coming, he will come as a warrior, ready to dispense wrath on the sinful.

And so, until he comes, we are commanded to wait with patience. James says as the farmer must wait patiently for the rain to make his grain grow, we must wait in the same way for Jesus Christ. After all, if we get in a hurry, nothing will really change other than we will just get upset.

There is another reason we must wait patiently. When we get antsy and nervous, we often tend to get irritable. This increases the likelihood of arguing with those around us. If we are patient and really depending on God, we will be less likely to cause any problems with fellow believers.

And we are warned in verse 9 that we do not know when the

LORD will come, and we do not want to have him come while we are sinning by arguing with a fellow believer! James says the arguer will be punished. Remember that the LORD is almost here – he could come at any time. Be on guard!

In verse 11, James uses the Old Testament story of Job as an example to follow. We have all heard the expression; *"The patience of Job,"* but we also know that Job was not very patient in our understanding of patience.

Job complained to his friends about what he was going through. He did not just sit quietly by as we think patience would dictate him to do. He went through losing everything in his life, including all of his children, all of his possessions, and then having a wife that could only tell him that he had it so bad he should just curse God and die!

But even as he went through this terrible time, and even though he complained, he keep solid faith in God, he did not curse God, nor did he question God's motives. And so, James uses this kind of patience as an example for us to have.

Since the book of JAMES does not follow one particular theme all the way through, it gives the reader the opportunity to learn a lot of things that James wants to pass on. We find one such subject in'

VERSE 12

"Above all, my brothers and sisters, do not swear - not by heaven or by earth or by anything else. All you need to say is a simple "Yes" or "No." Otherwise you will be condemned."

We have all heard others use the expression, *"I swear to God"* when they aren't even thinking about God. And we have heard much worse concerning using God's name, too. James is telling us to not swear at all!

He says all we need to do is simply give a yes or a no, but we should never elaborate and start swearing in any way. He means that Christians should not use oaths in ordinary speaking.

They should not call on heaven or earth as witnesses. They should not use the name of any other person in this way. The use of these is, in effect, appealing to the name of God. In the careless use of oaths, there is the danger of totally disrespecting the name of God.

EXODUS 20:7 [Holman Christian Standard Bible©]

"Do not misuse the name of the LORD your God, because the LORD will not leave anyone unpunished who misuses his name."

He says that those who do swear and take oaths in the name of God *will be condemned* before Almighty God. This message is so important, we are told what Jesus himself said about it.

MATTHEW 5:34-37

"34 But I tell you, do not swear an oath at all: either by heaven, for it is God's throne; 35 or by the earth, for it is his footstool; or by Jerusalem, for it is the city of the Great King. 36 And do not swear by your head, for you cannot make even one hair white or black. 37 All you need to say is simply 'Yes' or 'No'; anything beyond this comes from the evil one."

It is virtually the same message given to us in EXODUS. That is how important it is not to swear. Simply let your answer stand for itself. You do not have to prove anything you say to anyone you are talking. He says anything other than doing this comes only from Satan. Again, remember that to do this means we are inviting punishment upon ourselves.

VERSE 13-18

"13 Is anyone among you in trouble? Let them pray. Is anyone happy? Let them sing songs of praise. 14 Is anyone among you sick? Let them call the

elders of the church to pray over them and anoint them with oil in the name of the Lord. 15 And the prayer offered in faith will make the sick person well; the Lord will raise them up. If they have sinned, they will be forgiven. 16 Therefore confess your sins to each other and pray for each other so that you may be healed. The prayer of a righteous person is powerful and effective.

"17 Elijah was a human being, even as we are. He prayed earnestly that it would not rain, and it did not rain on the land for three and a half years. 18 Again he prayed, and the heavens gave rain, and the earth produced its crops."

If anyone is in trouble, the first thing that person should do is pray to God. The answer to that prayer may not remove the problem, but it will give help to give strength from God so that we can live through the trouble.

Those who are feeling good and are happy should praise God. They should sing praises of thanksgiving to God. James is reminding his readers to turn to God in both the good times and bad times. Prayer and praise are important parts in the lives of Christians.

1 THESSALONIANS 5:16-18 tells us what we should do.

"16 Rejoice always; 17 pray without ceasing; 18 in everything give thanks; for this is God's will for you in Christ Jesus."

We should always keep the LORD at the front of our minds and in the middle of our hearts, all the time. Verse 16 above tells us to rejoice in God always. We can all agree that God has done so much for us that we do not have any reason to not rejoice in his name.

Verse 17 tells us to always keep in prayer. When it dawns on you during the day that you are not in prayer – start praying again immediately! Do this every time you find that you are not praying!

And in verse 18 above, it instructs us to give thanks to God in every situation, not just the really good ones! It says this is Jesus' will for us to do.

James continues his instructions in verse 14. James tells his listeners that when they are ill, they are to ask the elders of the church to come and pray over them, and anoint the sick person with oil as they pray.

By doing that, we have been promised several things. Verse 15 says that when faithful men (the elders) pray faithful prayers over a sick person, God will not only heal the sick person, but will also forgive them of their sins.

The next verse says that we should confess our sins to one another. There is controversy on this statement. Some feel that we are to list all of our individual sins and confess them to other believers. Other people feel that we are to confess our individual sins to God as we commit them (or remember them) and to confess to God and to others that we are sinful creatures and need God's help and forgiveness.

Elijah was a prophet in the Old Testament. He prayed and asked God to send no rain on the land for $3\frac{1}{2}$ years. God honored that prayer. After that time, with no crops in between, he prayed that God would once again let it rain. And God honored that prayer, too. (see 1 KINGS 17:1 and 18:42-45).

What made his prayers so special? He believed that God would answer them. James says Elijah was an ordinary man. Well, we are ordinary men, too. All we need to be able to pray such serious prayers and get serious answers is to make sure we are right with God in the first place, and then to believe as we pray that God will answer the prayer.

Now, we also understand that God will answer your prayers in one of three ways. He will either say "YES", or He will say "NOT NOW", or he will say "NO".

If he says, "NO", he will give you understanding of why not. But the key is serious believing will beget serious answers.

And if a regular man like Elijah could do it, so can every other believer, if they simply choose to do it.

VERSES 19-20

"19 My brothers and sisters, if one of you should wander from the truth and someone should bring that person back, 20 remember this: Whoever turns a sinner from the error of their way will save them from death and cover over a multitude of sins."

It is possible for a person, who knows the truth about the *Lord Jesus, to turn away from him. This is not when a Christian does something wrong. It is more than that. It is when a person wanders away from Jesus Christ and denies the truth.

Christian brothers and sisters should look after one another. So, when one of them goes astray, the rest should feel deeply upset and try to gather that believer back. In fact, is it our Godly duty to try and persuade the one who left to come back to Jesus.

Now, supposing someone leaves and another believer brings that person back. He should know that God has saved that person who left from spiritual death. As that person comes back, God will forgive their sins.

about
JUDE

A Commentary
by
Pastor Bruce Ball

A continuation of the commentary on JAMES above.

Please see all permissions and ISBN on Title Page.

INTRODUCTION TO JUDE

This is a very short book, having virtually no chapters as it only consists of one page. But it will take some space here to go through it, because it has so many things Jude included for our understanding.

Have you ever heard the expression, *"Big things come in small packages?"* In the case of Jude, we will see how that statement is very true. Jude is a very short book, consisting of only one chapter (25 verses), but includes a plethora of information.

It was written by another of Jesus' half-brothers – Jude. It is the next to last book of the Bible, right before Revelation. And it is also one of the least-read and least-understood books in the New Testament. Even though this book is short and very unfamiliar, it is still the truth of God and chock-full of important information.

Let's start with the name. Jude is a variant of the name Judas. Ever since Judas Iscariot betrayed Jesus, the name has fallen out of favor. But before that, Judas was a very popular name among the Jews for two reasons.

First, Judas is the Greek version of the Hebrew name Judah. Secondly, Judas Maccabaeus was the name of a very famous Jewish revolutionary warrior who fought against the Greeks in the second century B.C.

The popularity of the name is reflected in there being 8 different men named Judas in the New Testament. But who is going to name a book of the New Testament "Judas"? That is why it is named "Jude".

In verse 1, it identifies the writer as *"Jude, a servant of Jesus Christ and a brother of James* He was an early church leader of great distinction and was also widely known as "James the Just." It is clear that he originally wanted to write a letter addressing another topic, (see verse 3), but instead, he ended up writing a warning about false teachers that had infiltrated the church.

It seems his readers were Jewish believers because he makes references to many Old Testament figures without any explanation of who they are. In addition to the Old Testament, he quotes and alludes to other religious writings that were well known at the time.

He uses many figures of speech taken from nature and he liked to write in triads. Notice the sets of three just in the opening verses. The book is written by; *James[1], a servant[2]*, and a *brother[3]*. It is written to the *called[1], loved[2]*, and *kept[3];* and he greets them with *mercy[1], peace[2]* and **love[3]**. As you read this very short book, see if you can find any other groupings of three.

If Jude seems vaguely familiar, like something else you have read recently, that is because it is very much like 2 Peter, especially the second chapter. They are so similar that it is assumed that one influenced the other. But did Jude influence Peter or did Peter influence Jude?

It is absolutely amazing how fast Satan works to destroy the works of God! Look how quickly God's church was inundated with false teachers and preachers! Just a few decades after Jesus' ascension back into Heaven, nearly every church was being attacked with these malicious and Satanic marauders. And if it came in that quickly after Jesus, it should come to no surprise that the same thing is happening today.

Let's begin our commentary, starting with verses 1-2.

JUDE

"¹ Jude, a servant of Jesus Christ and a brother of James; To those who have been called, who are loved in God the Father and kept for Jesus Christ: ² Mercy, peace and love be yours in abundance."

By the time Jude wrote this letter, most Jews understood the Greek language, so he had no problems writing in that language.

Jude was another brother who did not believe in Jesus as God before Jesus died upon the cross. But shortly after Jesus arose, he met with his family (see 1 CORINTHIANS 15:7). It was at that meeting that James became one of the first Christians (see ACTS 1:14).

So Jude does not want to sound pious by saying he is a brother of Jesus. He only says he is a brother of James – and that was only after he introduces himself as a servant to Jesus Christ.

When God puts a 'calling' on someone's heart, he is not just trying to get that person's attention. The 'calling' involves much more than that. God summons a person into duty, and that involves getting that person to dedicate the rest of their lives to God.

The Old Testament refers to God's care over his people as a 'Father'. (See Exodus 4:22-23 and Hosea 11:1).

But in the New Testament, Jesus shows us the complete meaning of God as 'Father' for an individual person. God sends sunshine and rain on good and bad people (See MATTHEW 5:44-45). But this does not mean that he is the 'Father' of everybody.

57

In the New Testament, the title 'Father' refers to the private and personal relation between God and each believer in Jesus (See JOHN 1:12-13 and EPHESIANS 2:4-8).

It involves giving that person a certain set of tasks to perform for the glory of God. And it also sets that person apart from the world so they can be a servant to the LORD. (See ROMANS 1:1).

God guards his people against Satan (the chief evil spirit – see 1 JOHN 5:18). God is keeping Christians safe for Jesus until he returns to this world (See JOHN 6:39 - 6:44 - 6:54; 1 CORINTHIANS 1:8; 1 THESSALONIANS 5:23 and 1 PETER 1:4).

God delights (is very pleased) to show pity (See MICAH 7:18). Christ himself is the Christian's great calm (See EPHESIANS 2:14). The Holy Spirit is the agent of love (See ROMANS 5:5).

In verse 2, we see James extending his Godly peace and love to them in his greeting. That will show the readers of his letter where his heart is focused; on God and then on other people. He loves the people and he does not want them to suffer.

VERSES 3-4

"*3 Dear friends, although I was very eager to write to you about the salvation we share, I felt compelled to write and urge you to contend for the faith that was once for all entrusted to God's holy people.*

4 For certain individuals whose condemnation was written about long ago have secretly slipped in among you. They are ungodly people, who pervert the grace of our God into a license for immorality and deny Jesus Christ our only Sovereign and Lord."

False teachers were creeping into the church and trying to

lead the people astray by upsetting the faith of Jude's readers (see verse 4).

So Jude is writing to urgently remind his readers to hold firmly to God by holding firm to what they have already been taught before.

In particular, they need rely more on God's love and remember to give sympathy instead of criticism or anger to their brothers and sisters in the faith. Love will keep them focused more on God and to each other. It will also help them to want to help others in need.

James number one goal here is to get the church to realize they have false teachers coming in to distort and destroy the truth of God's word and they need to protect themselves against them false teachers. (See ACTS 20:29-30). And Jude's readers need that knowledge and protection, because the words of the false teachers are a very real danger to them.

· In the original language, the word for 'urge' comes from the same origin as 'Comforter', which is a title for the Holy Spirit (See JOHN 14:16 and 14:26). The word 'comforter' actually means, *'one who comes near to help'*.

Although Jude cannot be with them himself, he is supporting his readers through his prayers.

· The 'truth' refers to the true person and work of Jesus Christ. The truth of Jesus Christ is the message that is often called the Gospel (the Good News) and refers to the plan of salvation that is available only through him and no place else.

Each Christian, from the very first one (Jude), has passed on this truth to other believers and now, Jude is re-emphasizing this message to his readers. They in turn must do the same for other people.

The New Testament often uses the expression 'certain men', to refer to a particular group of people. Teachers that travelled from one place to another often caused trouble in the first churches.

Jesus himself warned the people who followed him, warning them about false teachers

MATTHEW 7:15 shows how urgent this is for us to know.

"Beware of the false prophets, who come to you in sheep's clothing, but inwardly are ravenous wolves."

In 2 CORINTHIANS, chapters 10 and 11; Paul expounds on the seriousness of this subject.

So did Timothy in 1 TIMOTHY 4:1-2, and Peter gave the same message in 2 Peter 2:1-3. The Apostle John added his warning in 1 JOHN 4:1.

It is hard to identify the false teachers. They imitate genuine teachers. Some false teachers even become leaders or pastors in the church. But Jude will explain how their attitudes differ from the genuine teachers. And he will explain how dangerous the false teachers are. People might not easily recognize them, but God knows who they are, so their punishment is certain, and it will be very severe.

In Jude's day, many of the preachers travelled around and often spoke at different churches rather than staying in one church as most pastors do today.

Also, in every church age, Christians tend to be easily led as are sheep. We trust the pastor in front of us to be telling us the truth, and we want so desperately to be Godly ourselves, we believe everything the man says and how he delivers his message. And it is so easy to spread false teachings in that kind of environment.

But one failing many Christians have is that we hear what the teachers tell us and we immediately take it for granted that what we hear is absolutely correct. We are not to do that. We are to take what we hear and go into the bible to prove it right.

ACTS 17:11 [New Living Translation©] (Tyndale House©)

"And the people of Berea were more open-minded than those in Thessalonica, and they listened eagerly to Paul's message. They searched the Scriptures day after day to see if Paul and Silas were teaching them the truth."

That is what each Christian should be doing today, too – double checking to make sure that what the teacher says is gospel truth or lying truth.

If you take two pieces of rope, each one being 100 feet long, and one person holds one end of them one inch apart, and another person takes the other ends and holds them 3 inches apart, we barely notice the gap.

The false teaching starts out like the ropes. They are so close together the false teaching sounds just like the truth. But over time and distance, the difference gets wider and wider. Pretty soon, it has very little to do with God's precious truth.

And if we do not do our part to go into God's word ourselves and make sure it is the truth, then we are, in effect, perpetuating a false gospel. We are not to sit there and let someone regurgitate a message for us. We are to pay close attention and hold them responsible for what they teach.

Today, when you see or hear a teacher or pastor give you a message that is either all about your sending in money, or requesting if you send so much money in, God will bless you by blessing you with tons of money back – GET AWAY FROM HIM FAST! That is a false gospel.

Sure, ministries need money to operate, just as churches need money to help feed the people with supplies, chairs, and even food. But that should not be their main message, and it should never be for so much money that it puts the person and their families in financial jeopardy!

If you give your tithe and love offerings, God will bless you in the way that only he knows is best and only when he knows is the best timing for you to get it. All we need to do is be obedient to God's word and then be patient and trust him and wait.

VERSES 5-7

"5 Though you already know all this, I want to remind you that the Lord at one time delivered his people out of Egypt, but later destroyed those who did not believe. 6 And the angels who did not keep their positions of authority but abandoned their proper dwelling - these he has kept in darkness, bound with everlasting chains for judgment on the great Day. 7 In a similar way, Sodom and Gomorrah and the surrounding towns gave themselves up to sexual immorality and perversion. They serve as an example of those who suffer the punishment of eternal fire."

Of course, the Israelites were glad to be free from slavery and excited to be gone from Egypt. And God promised them their own country.

But the inhabitants of the country that God promised them were vast in number. And they were powerful. And they lived in strong cities. The Israelites did not trust God to help them to overcome the inhabitants of that country because they did what we do, and that is to focus first on the obstacle in front of us instead of going directly to God, in belief, and waiting for him to get rid of the obstacle for us.

We can pray in hope or in belief. We all hope God comes through for us, be not all of us really believe he will. God honors our belief, not our disbelief. So in the end, because of their disbelief, God let those Israelites die in the desert.

In verse 6, Jude mentions that some angels abandoned their heavenly positions and gave themselves over to evil against God. These, of course, were the fallen angels – the ones that knew what it was like to live in perfect surroundings, yet turned away from it. God had a special punishment for them.

Their pride was only one cause why those angels lost their place in God's kingdom. According to GENESIS 6:1-4, it seems that some of the wicked angels wanted to have sex with beautiful women on earth. Such an idea is bizarre to us. But the meaning is plain. Lust was the second cause why the wicked angels lost their proper place.

Jude combines the two sins when talking about the false teachers. They are guilty of pride and lust. Their pride wants them to have big churches and congregations, a lot of money in their money bags, or maybe they just want the fame that a TV show can bring them. But they have no Godly wisdom and their judgment from God will be as sure as the fate of the evil angels.

Because of the same sins, God destroyed the towns of Sodom and Gomorrah. (See GENESIS 19:1-25). The event made a permanent impression on the whole nation. In the Bible, there are 15 references to what happened in those towns. These references begin in the Book of Genesis and they continue to the end of the New Testament.

The towns called Sodom and Gomorrah were in a district that has masses of oil and gas, deep underground. Occasionally the gas and oil increased in pressure and a huge explosion would occur, spewing a lot of this gas and oil out into the air. As the burning oil pours down again, it destroys everything in its path. The heat is so powerful that the oil even burns on the surface of water, very similar to the ash of an active volcano will do.

This reaction of explosions sending hot oil into the sky along with many chunk of large rocks is what destroyed Sodom and Gomorrah. (See GENESIS 19:1-25). And it also destroyed other close-by towns in that region.

Some of the other towns in that region included and Zeboiim. (See DEUTERONOMY 29:23 and HOSEA 11:8). God saved a 5th town, called Zoar, because of Lot's prayer. (See GENESIS 19:20-22).

This event acts to remind us of what our future will be like if we entertain sin against God in our lives without wanting to repent (turn away from your current actions) and turn towards God.

Remember, we can never condone what God condemns and remain unpunished!

VERSE 8

"8 In the very same way, on the strength of their dreams these ungodly people pollute their own bodies, reject authority and heap abuse on celestial beings. 9 But even the archangel Michael, when he was disputing with the devil about the body of Moses, did not himself dare to condemn him for slander but said, "The Lord rebuke you!"

When we sin, we take in all kinds of sinful and negative things, even into our own bodies. We look at the instant pleasure we might derive from doing so, and ignore the long-term consequences of our actions.

When we do these things, and when we reject the spiritual authority over us, we do so with a heart of pride. Pride is a mortal sin against God.

PROVERBS 16:18 talks about what pride will do for you.

"Pride goes before destruction, a haughty spirit before a fall."

64

Those who do not care about living for Jesus Christ, or who even go so far as to belittle God or deny his very existence have prideful hearts and a very arrogant and snobby spirit. These two sins belong to those who will inhabit hell for all eternity.

Even the archangel Michael shows respect and submitted to the power of the devil. When he was confronted by Satan and Satan began arguing with Michael over Moses' body, Michael did not argue back. He showed his Godly heart and mind. He just told the devil, *"the LORD rebuke you."*

VERSE 10 [New Living Translation©] (Tyndale House©)

"But these people scoff at things they do not understand. Like animals who cannot think, they do whatever their instincts tell them to do, and so they end up bringing about their own destruction without even realizing what they are doing to themselves."

False teachers are like those described in verse 10 above. They prove they have no real understanding about spiritual matters in general, nor do they understand Gods plan in particular. (See 1 CORINTHIANS 2:7-16)

False teachers think they are important, but are really acting like raging animals who have no thinking ability.

2 PETER 2:1-3 describes them and their future in this manner.

"1 They will cleverly teach destructive heresies and even deny the Master who bought them. In this way, they will bring sudden destruction on themselves. 2 Many will follow their evil teaching and shameful immorality. And because of these teachers, the way of truth will be slandered. 3 In their greed they will make up clever lies to get hold of your money. But God condemned them long ago, and their destruction will not be delayed."

Some denominations have taken it upon themselves to rewrite parts of the bible; re-describe who God is and who Jesus is; and even reform the sacraments of marriage and baptism.

These church leaders will surely go to hell if unrepentant and are leading others down that same path because of their reprobate minds. That is why JAMES 3:1 tells us that many should not strive to be teachers because they will be judged by God in a more harsh way. To continue in this manner will ruin them in the end.

Jude is not warning about some terrible last illness, such as cancer or AIDS. He is writing about the certainty of the final judgement by God. Jude has already mentioned the fate of the Israelites in the desert in verse 5 and the fate of the towns called Sodom and Gomorrah in verse 7.

VERSE 11 shows us that they are blinded by their sinful ambition.

"What sorrow awaits them! For they follow in the footsteps of Cain, who killed his brother. Like Balaam, they deceive people for money. And like Korah, they perish in their rebellion."

In verses 5-7, Jude mentions three stories from the Old Testament. He used them to describe the wicked behavior of the false teachers in a general manner. But now, in verse 11, he uses three more Old Testament references in order to give personal examples of some of the things false teachers do to lie, cheat, and even try to kill someone spiritually.

Cain murdered his own brother (see GENESIS 4). Like Cain, the false teachers are destroying life. But in their case it is the spiritual life of people in the church. In other words, the false teachers are trying to ruin the church members' relation with God.

Originally, Balaam refused payment to announce an evil fate against the Israelites (See NUMBERS 22:7-18). But in the end, the offer of money became too strong and Balaam succumbed to the sin of receiving bribery. (See DEUTERONOMY 23:4).

Korah refused to accept the authority God had given to

Moses and Aaron. Korah and his followers all suffered an extraordinary death! (See NUMBERS chapter 16).

VERSES 12-13

"12 These people are blemishes at your love feasts, eating with you without the slightest qualm - shepherds who feed only themselves. They are clouds without rain, blown along by the wind; autumn trees, without fruit and uprooted - twice dead. 13 They are wild waves of the sea, foaming up their shame; wandering stars, for whom blackest darkness has been reserved forever."

Jude has compared the false teachers with certain Old Testament men who refused to obey God's laws. Now Jude repeats his attack on the false teachers in even more colourful language.

His word-pictures include the four regions of the physical world: Clouds in the air, Trees on the earth, Waves of the sea, and the Stars in the sky. All human activities, whether they be good and bad, affect everything else God has created. This is confirmed in ISIAH 24:5 and in JEREMIAH 12:4, below.

ISAIAH 24:5 [New Living Translation© (Tyndale House©)

"The earth suffers for the sins of its people, for they have twisted God's instructions, violated his laws, and broken his everlasting covenant."

JEREMIAH 12:4 also mentions how our sins help ruin creation.

"How long will the land lie dry and the grass? Because those who live in it are wicked, the animals and birds have perished. Moreover, the people are saying, "God will not see what we do or what will happen to us."

The original word for 'rocks' also means; 'spot' or 'stain'. Either of those three meanings would suit Jude's word picture accurately. The false teachers are like rocks that can destroy a ship. In other words, what the false teachers say can destroy a person's trust in God.

Or, Jude means the false teachers are like a dirty cloth. The fact that the false teachers are present at the special meal spoils the whole occasion. They are like the stain that ruins the cloth.

The 'love meal' was called the 'agape'. It was a special meal for all church members, whatever their class. Wealthy and poor members all ate together. Each person brought some food to share.

It is a Godly type of love. In most churches I have pastored, it is a regular site at these special meals to see the wealthier members actually preparing and serving the less wealthy members. And that is what it is all about; serving one another with love the same way our LORD Jesus came to serve us.

Paul knew that the standard of behaviour at the 'Agape' was sometimes not good (See 1 CORINTHIANS 11:17-20). This was certainly true about the church of Jude's readers. It seems that the church had a great many loyal members. They would not have noticed the quite arrival of the false teachers. So Jude's powerful words were necessary to warn the believers.

The false teachers are trying to use what should be an occasion for real Christian love. False words will ruin it, just like we read where other sins actually ruined the fields and everything else.

The behaviour of the false teachers is clearly and only in their self-interest. In other words, they care only about themselves. They have only come to feed themselves

In 1 CORINTHIANS 11:20-22, Paul talks of eating the Communion.

"20 So then, when you come together, it is not the Lord's Supper you eat, 21 for when you are eating, some of you go ahead with your own private suppers. As a result, one person remains hungry and another gets drunk.

^{22} Don't you have homes to eat and drink in? Or do you despise the church of God by humiliating those who have nothing? What shall I say to you? Shall I praise you? Certainly not in this matter!"

Paul was telling them that the Communion (or Lord's Supper) was a Godly meal, eaten with love for others and with compassion for others. Here, he is telling them that their own thought was on themselves and their having a good time.

He says some actually get drunk and few of them even wait on others. He scolds them and says he cannot praise them because of their actions and he basically tells them to leave and go home if they are going to act in such an ungodly way.

This practice had become commonplace. Another early Christian record called the Didache also refers to it.

The Didache is a book of teachings for the Apostles. It was written by the Apostle Peter to other Apostles. It was written about 96 A.D.

False teachers are like clouds without rain. They seem to offer good things. But they actually they have nothing beneficial to offer. All those "fake" clouds can do is to hide the light, and that only lasts temporarily. And all that the false teachers do is to lead people away from the true knowledge of God, but their demise from God is forthcoming so all they do is only for a short season.

Even as a wind blows clouds along, so the many words of the false teachers carry themselves along. In other words, their own ideas are too powerful for them to control. They simply continue with their speeches, which are totally without value.

The spirit of the false teachers is dead. So are their impressive words and loud voices. They cannot give real spiritual life to anybody, because they possess none themselves.

The false teachers are like certain trees in autumn. These trees have had a complete season to grow. By now much fruit should be making the branches heavy. But these trees have no fruit whatsoever. So the farmer destroys those trees.

MATTHEW 7:19 gives an illustration of what false teachers will get.

"Every tree that does not bear good fruit is cut down and thrown into the fire."

ISAIAH 57:20 also describes the false teachers.

"But those who still reject me are like the restless sea, which is never still but continually churns up mud, filth and dirt."

The bottom line is this: False teachers are working for Satan and are steadfast on his side. They oppose God for their own selfish desires and they have learned to speak as though they are for God. They are slick snack oil salesmen and are fooling millions of otherwise good Christians.

VERSES 14-15

"14 Enoch, the seventh from Adam, prophesied about them: "See, the Lord is coming with thousands upon thousands of his holy ones 15 to judge everyone, and to convict all of them of all the ungodly acts they have committed in their ungodliness, and of all the defiant words ungodly sinners have spoken against him."

The New Testament mentions Enoch in two other places. He appears: In LUKE 3:37 as an earlier member of the family of Jesus, and in HEBREWS 11:5 as an extraordinary example of a person who gives his full trust to God.

All those centuries ago, Enoch knew that one day the LORD would return in all divine glory and supremacy to this world.

Jude calls Enoch the seventh (7th) from Adam. There are five names between Adam and Enoch (see GENESIS 5:3-24 and 1 Chronicles 1:1-3). Jude includes the first and last names, as people did in ancient times.

Jews considered 'seven' to be the perfect number. 'Seven' meant something that was complete. As in the Sabbath.

GENESIS 2:2 talks about the seventh day.

"At the end of the sixth day, God had finished the work of creation and saw that it was good - so on the seventh day, he rested from all his work."

In Jude verse 9, he referred to wicked angels. They lost their place in heaven, because they would not accept God's plan for them. They refused to obey God.

The false teachers are like the wicked angels. The false teachers also refuse to obey God.

In the Old Testament, we hear from time to time about a man by the name of Enoch. He was a holy man who was so close to God, his life was considered to be "a walk with God." Enoch did not die. He went straight to heaven just like Elijah did.

GENESIS 5:24

"Enoch walked faithfully with God; then he was no more, because God took him away."

JUDE 15 tells about a future judgment when Jesus brings a vast number of angels with him when he comes back to judge the Earth.

About that judgment, MATTHEW 16:27 reads,

"For the Son of Man is going to come in his Father's glory with his angels, and then he will reward each person according to what they have done."

The angels are not there for any other reason than to serve Jesus as he acts as a judge to see God's final judgment play out. All people who have ever lived must attend this court to give account of their lives on earth. And then to receive judgement

JOHN 5:22

"Moreover, the Father judges no one, but has entrusted all judgment to the Son."

Jesus will then separate all of the people before him into two groups.

In MATTHEW 25:31-33, it shows how he will set up his court.

"31 When the Son of Man comes in his glory, and all the angels with him, he will sit on his glorious throne. 32 All the nations will be gathered before him, and he will separate the people one from another as a shepherd separates the sheep from the goats. 33 He will put the sheep on his right and the goats on his left."

When Jesus came before, he came as a peace-loving Saviour for all people. This time, he comes to cast judgment on every person who has ever lived. He will separate them into two groups; those who loved God (the sheep on his right), and those who rejected God. He will put those evil ones on his left (the goats.)

"34 "Then the King will say to those on his right, 'Come, you who are blessed by my Father; take your inheritance, the kingdom prepared for you since the creation of the world. 35 For I was hungry and you gave me something to eat, I was thirsty and you gave me something to drink, I was a stranger and you invited me in, 36 I needed clothes and you clothed me, I was sick and you looked after me, I was in prison and you came to visit me.'"

Jesus knows each person perfectly. There is a huge crowd in front of him. But Jesus can separate them into two groups without a mistake. We think it will be immediately, because Jesus knows each person perfectly. In fact, he knows them better than they know their selves.

Jesus will invite the God-loving sheep on his right into heaven, into the place that has been prepared for them. On his special seat of glory, Jesus signals to his angels where each person is to go. Into the group on his left. Or into the group on his right.

On that day, no genuine Christian will be mixed in the mass of wicked people. Nor will the cleverest of wicked people be able to hide in the mass of Christians.

Jude repeats the word 'wicked' to emphasise that the fate of the false teachers is certain. And that the judgement is against every part of their lives.

At this point, there is no longer any class of people There is no more difference between rulers or those who are ruled over, no between kings and servants, nor between ranks or even between churches and denominations.

All of these distinctions will have been ended permanently. Every person will be judged by Jesus Christ on the basis of what they have personally done and felt on an individual basis, not on anything else.

After giving a brief explanation as to why he saved the sheep, he turns his attention to the evil and wicked ones on his left. He tells them to get out of his sight and to go to the lake of fire where they will spend eternity. And he gives them a brief explanation as to why he considers them evil.

"41 Then he will say to those on his left, 'Depart from me, you who are cursed, into the eternal fire prepared for the devil and his angels. 42 For I was hungry and you gave me nothing to eat, I was thirsty and you gave me

nothing to drink, [43] *I was a stranger and you did not invite me in, I needed clothes and you did not clothe me, I was sick and in prison and you did not look after me.'"*

VERSE 16

"These people are grumblers and faultfinders; they follow their own evil desires; they boast about themselves and flatter others for their own advantage."

Jude now describes the evilness of false teachers. They are as bitter to God as anything could be. They are the worst of the worst of the worst, for they have taken truth and twisted it into an unrecognizable lie – all to get what they want, which is usually money or fame!

Long ago the Israelites were slaves under brutal condition in Egypt, but after 400 years, they all began praying for God's help in saving them. What did God do? When it dawned on the entire nation of Jews to rely on God, he rescued them by leading them out of captivity and into the freedom of the deserts, where they were to go to the Promised Land that he had given them in the past.

As humans, we tend to have one very fatal flaw; we think we must understand fully understand something before we give it our stamps of approval. We cannot do that with God, we must sit back and willingly obey him and let him do good things in his timing and in his way.

Even after God freed them from captivity, the Israelites began griping because God led them into the desert. There was no water for them to drink. (See EXODUS 15:24; 17:3 and NUMBERS 14:29).

I live in the Sonoran Deserts of southern Arizona and I can personally attest to the fact that drinking water is needed to stay alive in the heat of the desert. In the heat of the summer, one can suffer heat stroke if left in the full sun without water for more than 20-30 minutes. It can be brutal.

But rather than to trust in God and wait for the right timing to get water, the Israelites complained: *'God ought to realize and care about the plight we are in!'*

Human character does not change. Lucian taught philosophy in the second century AD. He writes about the same sort of attitude, even back then:

> 'Nothing that happens ever satisfies you! You complain about everything. You do not want what you possess. Your only desire is for what you do not have. In winter, you wish it was summer. In summer, you wish it was winter. You are like some sick people. You cannot please them. Nothing is right. Everything is wrong!'

Such selfish people think only about themselves. They have no interest in what someone else may need. It is that old quirk of our nature showing up again and again: *I want what I want, I want it now, or I will get upset!*

In VERSES 17-19, Jude starts talking about people who divide.

"17 But, dear friends, remember what the apostles of our Lord Jesus Christ foretold. 18 They said to you, "In the last times there will be scoffers who will follow their own ungodly desires." 19 These are the people who divide you, who follow mere natural instincts and do not have the Spirit."

He reminds them of what previous apostles have taught; that in the Last Days, there will be those who are evil to the core and they will scoff at all Godly things, and they will do all they can to separate people apart from each other. And like all wicked people, they will do this for their own selfish (and sometimes outright crazy) desires. Jude even goes so far as to say they have no spirit!

In VERSE 17, Jude changes his tone. He writes; '... *dear friends'.*

We know he is talking to his Christian brothers and sisters now because he calls them 'friends'. The false teachers are no longer Jude's immediate subject.

Jude now turns from his collection of Old Testament references (Go back and read VERSES 5-16). There are more recent people that warned about the unwelcome arrival of false teachers in the church, and he begins talking about what they said.

Jesus himself had even given warnings to his friends that wicked people were sure to try and turn other people away from God.

First, in MARK 13:5-6, Jesus gave this warning;

"Watch out that no one deceives you. 6 Many will come in my name, claiming, 'I am he,' and will deceive many."

He gives another warning in MARK 13:21-22;

"21 At that time if anyone says to you, 'Look, here is the Messiah!' or, 'Look, there he is!' do not believe it. 22 For false messiahs and false prophets will appear and perform signs and wonders to deceive, if possible, even the elect."

He says many evil imposters will even have the Satanic give gifts of performing miracles, just to make people think they are the One. Jesus warns us to NOT BELIEVE THEM!

Any time the bible repeats itself over and over again, we know the point it is making is a very serious one that we need to be very aware of and to follow their lead! Just like other disciples had declared the same message in their teachings. For examples;

In ACTS 20:28-31b Luke (the writer of ACTS) gives this warning,

"28 Keep watch over yourselves and all the flock of which the Holy Spirit has made you overseers. Be shepherds of the church of God, which he bought with his own blood. 29 I know that after I leave, savage wolves will come in among you and will not spare the flock. 30 Even from your own number men will arise and distort the truth in order to draw away disciples after them. 31 So be on your guard!"

To all church leaders, he chides them to constantly keep a close watch over themselves and the members of the church that are under their care. He reminds them that God's Holy Spirit put them in that position and they have a duty to honor him.

And then he says that after he leaves, these savage and evil wolves will come into leadership of the church (teachers), many from within their own ranks and be accepted!

He says their only ambition is to lead the church astray using half-truths and total lies so that people will follow them instead of Jesus Christ. And then in verse 31, he begins by uttering a very dire warning: "So, be on your guard!"

Notice that when the bible uses exclamation points, it does so for no other reason than to get your full attention on something vitally urgent!

God loves to have order in his creation. One way he does this is to set up a hierarchy which keeps things focused. He has given his authority to the apostles to be part of the hierarchy.

But he has also given them an obligation to perform their duties so that all glory points to Jesus Christ as God's only begotten Son, and to find in him the ONLY way to salvation and heaven. This is verified in the following verses:

In JOHN 14:6, Jesus declares;

"I am the way and the truth and the life. No one comes to the Father - except through me."

Again, in 1 JOHN 2:22-23, Jesus sets the record straight.

"22 And who is a liar? Anyone who says that Jesus is not the Christ and Saviour. Anyone who denies the Father and the Son is an antichrist. 23 Anyone who denies the Son doesn't have the Father, either. But anyone who acknowledges the Son as the only path to heaven has the Father also."

So now, all we have to decide is whether we want to believe in the bible as truth or do we choose not to believe in it as truth? Do we understand that we cannot cherry-pick what parts of it we want to believe (the comfortable parts), or do we choose to believe it as 100% truth from cover to cover?

Many people say they cannot believe in it fully because there are too many contradictions in it. First of all, there are no contradictions in the bible. If there is something in it that we cannot understand, that just means we do not understand it, but it does not mean that the bible is not accurate.

Most of us cannot understand how a couple tons of metal can fly through the air like a bird, but we know that when fashioned in the shape of an airplane, it can fly high and fast. Even though we do not understand that, we know and believe in it as truth.

Believing the bible is the same. We do not believe by sight, but only by faith in God Almighty, through Jesus Christ the Son.

In JUDE, verse 18, we can see that people who laugh at holy matters consider them a joke. Such people have no place for God in their lives. And they have little or no thought for other people. Their hearts and minds are only focused on their own silly, immature and evil desires!

They love to believe that they have are knowledgeable, intelligent and even have influence over others that need and deserve to be looked up to. Their great desire is for people to think of them as important.

These people are the most ignorant of all people when it comes to any kind of wisdom or understanding.

Going further, Jude say these men divide Christians in a church. Believe it or not, that is their goal and they find delight in causing this chaos. They form groups that disagree with one another. They upset people. They offer no real compassion or love to anyone, because they truly have no spirit. To them it is all a gigantic put-on; nothing with them is real except for their wickedness.

VERSES 20-23

"20 But you, dear friends, by building yourselves up in your most holy faith and praying in the Holy Spirit, 21 keep yourselves in God's love as you wait for the mercy of our Lord Jesus Christ to bring you to eternal life.

"22 Be merciful to those who doubt; 23 save others by snatching them from the fire; and to others show mercy, mixed with fear - hating even the clothing stained by corrupted flesh."

Drawing his letter to a close, Jude again addresses his listeners and readers as 'friends'. He urges them to build themselves up in God's Holy Spirit and praying in the Spirit, all in the love of God while we wait for Jesus' return to escort us into heaven.

He says we should not hate unbelievers but to have mercy on them because they either have never been shown the truth, or they just do not have the ability to understand the truth for a variety of reason.

He says to lead everyone we can to salvation through Jesus Christ. When he says to show mercy to others, that is exactly what he means. And there is no way we can feel mercy, or even show it, if we do not have the love of fellow human in our hearts.

And when he speaks of having 'fear', it is the fear of what will happen to our souls if we do not receive Jesus as our Saviour.

GENERAL QUESTIONS & ANSWERS

When talking about Godly love, do not confuse that with 'liking' a person. Liking a person is when you enjoy that person's company and love to be around them. They are pleasant. And it is very good to like people, but we do not hang around those who have rejected Jesus, except to lead them back.

Keeping in mind that we, as followers of Christ, are never to show hate towards anyone for any reason, and we are not to be rude, even if we disagree with them. But we are commanded to keep ourselves safe from earthly corruption.

Consider this your deepest held beliefs and thoughts. I implore you to not just quickly read through the following, but to test yourself to see where you really do stand in these.

Do you feel called by the very holy name by God to be drawn to him? Do you believe that?

Have you received, and are living, the faith that our bible teaches you should have? Have you ever had one-on-one talks with God, asking him to specifically ask him to help you have that kind of true and deep faith?

Do you really believe that God thought about you before the foundations of the world were laid? That He planned your life long before you were even born? (See PSALM 139)

And, EPHESIANS 1:4 [New Living Translation©] (Tyndale House©)

"Even before he made the world, God loved us and chose us - in Christ - to be holy and without fault in his eyes."

If you truly believe that, because of your personal relationship with Jesus Christ, you belong to a royal priesthood of God, and then you will keep yourself separate from all the evil in this world.

You have nothing to fear from what people think and say about you, you are God's. Take comfort in what my father used to tell my brothers and me: 'If people are talking about you, they have one very good subject to talk about.'

You can keep yourself separate from the ugly spirits that want to draw you down to the base level of this world.

2 CORINTHIANS 6:14-18 [New Living Translation© (Tyndale House©)

"14 Don't team up with those who are unbelievers. How can righteousness be a partner with wickedness? How can light live with darkness? 15 What harmony can there be between Christ and the devil? How can a believer be a partner with an unbeliever? 16 And what union can there be between God's temple and idols? For we are the temple of the living God. As God said: "I will live in them and walk among them. I will be their God, and they will be my people.

"17 Therefore, come out from among unbelievers, and separate yourselves from them, says the LORD. Don't touch their filthy things, and I will welcome you. 18 And I will be your Father, and you will be my sons and daughters, says the LORD Almighty."

This passage is not telling us to ignore non-believers. It is saying that while we ae in this world, we must live in it, too – but we are not to be 'of' this world. When associating with non-believers, we must set ourselves as a Christian example of love and joy, not being afraid to do so.

Just as there can be no merging between worldly habits and beliefs (which are from Satan) and joining them to Christ's beliefs (which are all Godly), there can be no teaming up with unlike partners in any relationship without risking our own salvation! Remember the true old analogy of just one rotten apple in a barrel of good apples. Over time the good apples will not make the rotten one good, but the one rotten one will make all the good ones bad.

As a Christian, we want God to always walk with us. But if we enter into ungodly relationships, or frequent ungodly places just to enjoy ourselves, then how can we expect a holy God to go there with us?

When he says to separate ourselves from them, again, he is not saying to shun them. He is saying that to have a right relationship with them, and if they have no accepted Jesus Christ, then associate with them on a Christian level, but do not become part of what they are at present. Be their leader, not their follower.

You can go through life wearing this knowledge like a crown: You are an eternal spirit, chosen by God and in his eyes, you are preciously created for heavenly things. Then the things of this world lose their appeal, because their darkness and deceit are exposed to you. He has called you into His marvellous light. And if you choose to do so, you can do it!

You are in this world, and you have to interact with it. At school, at work, wherever you are, you will meet situations that cause you to be tempted. But if you have this constant awareness that you have a high and holy calling it gives you the power to:

Walk away from filthy conversations, or gossip, or backbiting. You have the ability to be an individual in Christ without feeling you need to cave in to other people's desires for you.

Be respectful, kind, and loving when everyone else around you is not. We are called to give respect to all of those in authority over us, whether we agree with them or not. This includes our teachers, bosses, co-workers, parents, or whoever else you have to associate with in your day-to-day life

ROMANS 12:21 reminds us to repay with goodness what you might get from others that is bad or evil. Do not return evil for evil.

Live before God's face is right in front of you, looking at you with each decision you make during your day, but do not worry about what others say to you, or about you, as you make those decisions. In your eternity, only God counts, those around you do not.

Instead of worrying about what people think of you be bold and courageous. Every time you take undo criticism because you choose to stand for God instead of caving in to other, you build yourself stronger in the LORD.

PHILIPPIANS 2:15

"That you may become blameless and harmless, children of God without fault in the midst of a crooked and perverse generation, among whom you shine as lights in the world."

One last question, and please thing about this.

How do you think you would feel if you were before Jesus on your day of judgment and he asked you why you did not try to influence a particular non-believer you knew, and just chose to be his friend instead? What answer would you give Jesus, other than feeling totally ashamed of yourself?

And then, how would you feel if Jesus told you that because you did not try and reach him, that friend of yours went to hell?

Maybe we should all take advantage of our lives now to do what God wants us to do, rather than be caught up in that question and answer routine from Jesus!

I love you in Christ. Love is not the same thing as 'liking'. Love is when you want desperately to make sure you do everything in your power to keep someone from going to hell.

ABOUT THE AUTHOR

Pastor Bruce Ball was raised in a blue-collar Christian household. He was born in Arizona, but at the age of six, his family moved back to the Appalachian Mountains of Jonesville, Virginia. Shortly thereafter, he received Jesus as his Savior and told his parents he wanted to preach.

Pastor Bruce, with the help of the LORD and his wife Diana, has planted two churches and pastored three other churches during his career.

Each step of the way, they both remained focused on pursuing God on purpose and the need to tell others about the loving plan of salvation through Jesus Christ.

They teach it is not about following the traditions of legalism or just the rules of God, but the giving over of your heart to Jesus Christ as your own personal Savior and then living your life according to His desires for you and not following your own desires in life – all because that is your new desire in him.

Pastor Bruce and his wife Diana have three grown children, five grandchildren, and are currently living in the Sonoran Desert of southern Arizona. They are active in their local church, preaching and teaching to all who will listen.

His advice to everyone is, *"If Jesus died for us back then, shouldn't we be living for Him today?"*

37728846R00055

Made in the USA
Middletown, DE
01 March 2019